CHRISTMAS TRIVIA

CHRISTMAS
TRIVIA
200 FUN & FASCINATING FACTS ABOUT CHRISTMAS

Jennie Miller Helderman & Mary Caulkins

GRAMERCY BOOKS
NEW YORK

This 2002 edition is published by Gramercy Books, an imprint of Random House Value Publishing, a division of Random House, Inc., New York, by arrangement with Crane Hill Publishers, Birmingham, Alabama.

Gramercy is a registered trademark and the colophon is a trademark of Random House, Inc.

Random House
New York • Toronto • London • Sydney • Auckland
www.randomhouse.com

Printed in Singapore

Library of Congress Cataloging -in-Publication Data
Helderman, Jennie.
    Christmas trivia : 200 fun & fascinating facts about Christmas / Jennie Miller
  Helderman & Mary Caulkins.
        p. cm.
    Caulkins's name appears first on the earlier edition.
    Originally published: Birmingham, AL : Crane Hill Publishers, c1998.
    ISBN 0-517-22070-9
    1. Christmas—Miscellanea. 2. Questions and answers. I. Caulkins, Mary. II. Title.
GT4985 .H344 2002
394.2663—dc21   2002069281

9 8 7 6 5 4 3 2

CHRISTMAS TRIVIA

THE ANSWERS BEGIN ON PAGE 85

1. When did December 25 become the date to celebrate Christmas?
   a. The day Jesus was born
   b. A.D. 336
   c. July 4, 1776
   d. 4 B.C.

2. Where did the real Saint Nicholas live?
   a. Jerusalem
   b. London
   c. Holland
   d. Turkey

3. When did Saint Nicholas live?
   a. 4 B.C.
   b. Fourth century A.D.
   c. Middle Ages
   d. Renaissance

4. How many animals were present at the manger where Jesus was born?

5. Which Old Testament prophet named Bethlehem as the site of the Messiah's birth?

6. Who put Saint Nicholas in prison, and who freed him?
   a. Merlin, then King Arthur
   b. Herod, then Saint Peter
   c. Roman emperor Diocletian, then Constantine
   d. Machiavelli, then the de Médicis

7. In what year do many scholars think Jesus was born?
   a. 4 B.C.
   b. The year 0
   c. The year 1
   d. A.D. 4

8. Who told Mary she was expecting a baby?
   a. Luke, the physician
   b. Joseph
   c. Gabriel
   d. John the Baptist

9. Where in the Bible can you read the Christmas story?
   a. Matthew, Mark, Luke, and John
   b. Matthew and Luke
   c. Mark and Luke
   d. The Old Testament

10. What were the names of the wise men?
    a. Peter, Paul, and Simon
    b. Peter, Paul, and Mary
    c. Malachi, Beelzebub, and Caspian
    d. Melchior, Balthasaar, and Kaspar

11. What holiday did the ancient Romans celebrate on
    December 25?
    a. Copernicus
    b. Saturnalia
    c. Demetrius
    d. All Caesar Day

12. How many wise men were there?

13. What are the Twelve Days of Christmas?

14. Little children look to Saint Nicholas as their patron saint. Who else claims him as patron saint?
    a. Bankers and pawnbrokers
    b. Sailors and travelers
    c. Merchants and thieves
    d. All of the above

15. In what country did the Christmas tree originate?

16. What two countries have adopted Saint Nicholas
    as their patron saint?
    a. Holland and Germany
    b. Italy and Greece
    c. Greece and Russia
    d. England and Holland

17. How did Saint Nicholas help three young girls to get married?
    a. He gave them the gift of beauty.
    b. He gave them each a dowry.
    c. He introduced them to handsome young princes.
    d. He gave them three frogs to kiss.

18. Frankincense is a sweet spice. What is myrrh?
    a. An aromatic resin once used in burials
    b. A precious jewel
    c. A spice to preserve meat
    d. The first fruitcake

19. The word Yule has Scandinavian origins and comes
    from the old word Jol. What does it mean?
    a. Reindeer
    b. A log
    c. A festival
    d. Strudel

20. What advice did Pope Gregory the Great give in A.D. 601 regarding pagan customs?
    a. Rid them from God's earth.
    b. Burn all pagans at the stake.
    c. Adapt them to the praise of God.
    d. Record them for scholars.

21. What happened to Saint Nicholas in the year 1087?
    a. He moved to Holland.
    b. His bones were moved to Italy.
    c. His beard turned white.
    d. He was buried in Bethlehem.

22. Legend attributes the first celebration of Christmas in England to whom?

    a. Hadrian
    b. Robin Hood
    c. King Richard the Lionhearted
    d. King Arthur

23. Mistletoe is said to bring happiness, safety, and good fortune unless what happens?

    a. It touches the ground.
    b. It has red berries.
    c. Its berries drop off.
    d. The berries turn brown.

24. What does holly signify?

25. What is a yule log?

26. What is wassail?

27. The word wassail comes from the Anglo-Saxon waes hael,
    which means
    a. Witch hazel
    b. Wise owl
    c. Be well
    d. Beware

28. What did Merlin the Magician request of God on Christmas day?

29. What is the significance of December 6?
    a. It is the feast day of Saint Nicholas.
    b. It is Boxing Day.
    c. It is the feast day of Saint Stephen.
    d. It is the birthday of Saint Patrick.

30. Charlemagne was crowned Holy Roman Emperor by Pope Leo III on Christmas Day in the year 800. Who was crowned on Christmas Day in the year 1066?

31. Who was the first to have a nativity scene at Christmas?
    a. Constantine the Great
    b. Pope Gregory
    c. Saint Francis of Assisi
    d. Saint Nicholas

32. What did the Della Robbias in Florence, Italy, make during the early Renaissance?
    a. Marzipan
    b. Enameled Christmas decorations
    c. Frescoes
    d. Fruitcakes

33. On Christmas Day, 1492, Christopher Columbus
    a. Set sail for the New World
    b. Kissed Queen Isabella under the mistletoe
    c. Landed in Cuba
    d. Named a port in Haiti

34. Who, according to tradition, had the first Christmas tree?
    a. Charles Dickens
    b. Charlemagne
    c. Martin Luther
    d. Beowulf

35. One of Botticelli's final works was a nativity scene.
    What is it called?
    a. *Mary Rising from the Manger*
    b. *Bethlehem in Gloria Excelsis*
    c. *The Nativity of the Shepherds*
    d. *The Mystic Nativity*

36. How many times in all his works does William Shakespeare use the word "Christmas"?
    a. 3
    b. 13
    c. 33
    d. 103

37. In what play does Shakespeare talk about the time so hallowed "—no spirit dare stir abroad . . . no planets strike . . . "?

a. *Macbeth*
b. *Hamlet*
c. *King Lear*
d. *The Tempest*

38. Legend has it that a student of Queens College, Oxford, was attacked by a wild boar on Christmas Day. What did he use to choke the boar?

a. A yule log
b. His copy of "Aristotle"
c. Excalibur
d. A bough of mistletoe

39. Why did town criers in England in the 1640s shout
"No Christmas! No Christmas!"?
a. The calendar changed, and it was not December.
b. Christmas was illegal.
c. The grinch stole Christmas.
d. Scrooge told them to do it.

40. What well-known English physicist was born on Christmas Day
in 1642?
a. John Locke
b. Jonathan Kepler
c. Sir Isaac Newton
d. William Harvey

41. What are the four weeks prior to Christmas called?

42. What did Little Jack Horner do to the Christmas pie?

43. What is thought to be the oldest Christmas carol?

44. December 25, 1620, was the Pilgrims' first Christmas in the New World. How did these devout people spend it?
    a. Cutting trees
    b. Fasting and praying
    c. Feasting with the Indians
    d. Mumming

45. What carol is often set to a melody from a Handel opera?
    a. "It Came Upon a Midnight Clear"
    b. The Hallelujah Chorus of Handel's Messiah
    c. "While Shepherds Watched Their Flocks"
    d. Luther's "Cradle Song"

46. Why do children put out stockings or shoes to receive gifts from Santa?
    a. Santa's first gifts accidentally landed in stockings.
    b. Their stockings are small, so they don't appear greedy.
    c. Santa abhors cold feet.
    d. The custom began with ancient pagans.

47. Who are "Saint Nicholas's clerks"?
    a. Bookkeepers
    b. Thieves
    c. Lawyers
    d. Scribes

48. Why are pawnbrokers indebted to Saint Nicholas?
    a. He gives them his leftover toys to sell.
    b. He brings them gifts, like he does for children.
    c. He taught them to keep ledgers.
    d. He gave them their symbol.

49. Where did the name "Kris Kringle" come from?
   a. A crunchy German cereal
   b. German Protestant churches
   c. A medieval king in Bavaria
   d. A Teutonic legend

50. What Christmas hymn written in 1719 paraphrases Psalm 98?
   a. "Te Deum"
   b. "Joy to the World"
   c. "All My Heart This Night Rejoices"
   d. "Jeremiah Rana Catesbeiana"

51. Who composed *The Christmas Oratorio*, performed for the
first time in 1734 in Leipzig?

    a. Johann Sebastian Bach
    b. Felix Mendelssohn
    c. Ludwig van Beethoven
    d. George Fredrick Handel

52. What was the figurehead on the *Goede Vrouw*, the ship bring-
ing the first colonists from the Netherlands to
New Amsterdam?

    a. The Virgin Mary
    b. The Christmas Lily
    c. Saint Nicholas
    d. There was no figurehead.

53. Who wrote "Hark! The Herald Angels Sing"?
    a. Charles Wesley
    b. Martin Luther
    c. Sir Walter Raleigh
    d. Unknown

54. What traditional Christmas musical work was first performed in Dublin on April 13, 1742?
    a. "Greensleeves"
    b. *The Nutcracker*
    c. *The Christmas Oratorio*
    d. *The Messiah*

55. What did George Washington do on Christmas Day, 1776?
    a. He ate beans with his troops at Valley Forge.
    b. He crossed the Delaware River.
    c. He ate Christmas dinner with Martha.
    d. He listened to Francis Scott Key's new song.

56. New York's *Tory Royal Gazette* advertised Christmas toys in 1777. What were they?
    a. Toy soldiers
    b. Porcelain dolls
    c. Teddy bears
    d. Whirligigs

57. What Protestant church was founded on Christmas Eve early in the history of the United States?

   a. Presbyterian
   b. Congregational
   c. Baptist
   d. Methodist

58. Who was the first president to spend Christmas in the White House?

   a. George Washington
   b. James Madison
   c. John Adams
   d. Thomas Jefferson

59. Who first described Santa as a cheerful, rotund fellow riding through the air in a sleigh drawn by reindeer?
   a. Washington Irving
   b. Nathaniel Hawthorne
   c. James Fenimore Cooper
   d. Henry Wadsworth Longfellow

60. What treaty ending a U.S. war was signed on Christmas Eve?
   a. The Treaty of Versailles
   b. The Treaty of Appomattox
   c. The Treaty of Ghent
   d. The Pentagon Papers

61. What American frontiersman was born in Kentucky on Christmas Eve, 1809?

a. Kit Carson
b. Daniel Boone
c. Jim Bowie
d. Meriwether Lewis

62. What resulted when the organ broke down in Saint Nicholas's Church in a small Austrian village near Salzburg on Christmas Eve in 1818?

a. The song "I Heard the Bells on Christmas Day"
b. The hand bell choir gave a concert.
c. The carol "Silent Night"
d. John Calvin preached the Christmas sermon.

63. Who wrote "The Night Before Christmas"?
   a. Samuel Clemens
   b. Washington Irving
   c. William Makepeace Thackeray
   d. Clement C. Moore

64. How many times does Moore refer to Santa Claus?
   a. None
   b. One
   c. Three
   d. Seven

65. Name Santa's reindeer.

66. What happened when Saint Nicholas laughed?

67. What visions danced in the children's heads?

68. Where is the natural home of the poinsettia?
    a. Mexico
    b. Florida
    c. California
    d. Australia

69. Where did the poinsettia get its name?
    a. From an Indian princess
    b. From a Spanish explorer
    c. From Columbus's navigator
    d. From a United States diplomat

70. What does December 25, 1821, mean to the American Red Cross?
    a. The date of its founding
    b. The birth date of founder William Booth
    c. The birth date of founder Clara Barton
    d. The end of the Crimean War

71. What is the original meaning of the word *carol*?
    a. A prayerful song
    b. A song to dance to
    c. A Gregorian chant
    d. The music of bells

72. Where and when were Christmas cards first produced?
    a. Boston in 1818
    b. London in 1843
    c. St. Louis in 1814
    d. A drugstore in the Bronx in 1892

73. Who popularized the Christmas tree in England?
    a. Charles Dickens
    b. Ebenezer Scrooge
    c. Prince Albert
    d. John Wesley

74. Which was the first state to make Christmas
    an official holiday?
    a. Massachusetts
    b. Rhode Island
    c. Virginia
    d. Alabama

75. What is the name of Scrooge's deceased business partner
    in Charles Dickens's *A Christmas Carol*?

76. In *A Christmas Carol*, who hosted a ball?
    a. Ebenezer
    b. Fezziwig
    c. Charles Dickens
    d. Tiny Tim

77. What did Tiny Tim's family have for Christmas dinner?
    a. A turkey
    b. Venison
    c. A goose
    d. Cold porridge

78. What popular Christmas song was actually written as a generic wintertime song for a Sunday School program?
    a. "Jingle Bells"
    b. "Winter Wonderland"
    c. "Over the Hills and through the Woods"
    d. "Here We Come a Wassailing"

79. Which Christmas carol is based on Matthew 2:1-12?
    a. "While Shepherds Watched Their Flocks"
    b. "It Came Upon a Midnight Clear"
    c. "We Three Kings"
    d. "Hark! The Herald Angels Sing"

80. Who asked cartoonist and illustrator Thomas Nast to draw an image of Santa Claus?
    a. Norman Rockwell
    b. Abraham Lincoln
    c. Charles Dickens
    d. Henry Wadsworth Longfellow

81. What do Santa Claus, the Democratic donkey, and the Republican elephant have in common?
    a. The same man created their images.
    b. They all appeared on a ballot in the 1860s.
    c. They were each inspired by a poem.
    d. Nothing

82. Who was the first president to have a Christmas tree in the White House?
    a. Abraham Lincoln
    b. Jefferson Davis
    c. Franklin Pierce
    d. Andrew Jackson

83. Henry Wadsworth Longfellow penned "Christmas Bells" on Christmas Day during the Civil War. What Christmas song did the poem become?
    a. "Silver Bells"
    b. "Jingle Bells"
    c. "I Heard the Bells on Christmas Day"
    d. "Peace on Earth, Good Will to Men"

84. What did General Sherman give Abraham Lincoln for Christmas in 1864?
    a. The burning of Atlanta
    b. Tara
    c. Savannah
    d. The Chattanooga Choo-Choo

85. What is meant by a Christmas carol that is "macaronic"?
   a. It is of Italian origin.
   b. It freely mixes English and Latin.
   c. It is a weighty tune.
   d. It can be combined with havarti.

86. In "Away in a Manger," what are the cattle doing?

87. Which Christmas song quieted the trench warfare in the Franco-Prussian War in 1870?
   a. "Silent Night"
   b. "The First Noel"
   c. "O Holy Night"
   d. "Gloria in Excelsis Deo"

88. "What Child Is This?" is sung to what tune?

89. Who was first in the United States to have electric lights on a Christmas tree?
    a. Thomas Edison
    b. The vice president of the electric light company
    c. Alexander Graham Bell's neighbor
    d. John Jacob Astor

90. Who was first in the White House to have electric lights on a Christmas tree?
    a. Grover Cleveland
    b. Teddy Roosevelt
    c. Chester Arthur
    d. Herbert Hoover

91. What is engelshaar?

    a. A musical term
    b. An Austrian dessert
    c. Angel's hair
    d. An electric Christmas decoration

92. Who was the father of the American Christmas card?

    a. N. C. Wyeth
    b. Winston Hallmark
    c. Winslow Homer
    d. Louis Prang

93. Whose work included a North Pole address for Santa Claus?
    a. Mark Twain
    b. O. Henry

    c. Thomas Nast
    d. Christina Rosetti

94. Mrs. Claus was a character in Katherine Lee Bates's 1889 book, *Goody Santa Claus on a Sleigh Ride*. What else did Bates write?
    a. *Frankenstein*
    b. "America the Beautiful"

    c. *A Very Merry Cricket*
    d. *Godey's Lady's Book*

95. How did Vincent Van Gogh spend Christmas Eve, 1888?
    a. Sailing to Tahiti
    b. Completing his masterpiece, *Starry Night*
    c. Painting *Sunflowers* in one sitting
    d. Cutting off his left earlobe

96. Engelbert Humperdinck wrote an opera that is traditionally performed at Christmas, although it has nothing to do with the holiday. What is the opera called?
    a. *Hansel and Gretel*
    b. *The Nutcracker*
    c. *Madame Butterfly*
    d. *The Messiah*

97. Which newspaper ran the "Yes, Virginia" editorial?
    a. *The New York Times*
    b. *The New York Sun*
    c. *The Boston Globe*
    d. *The Washington Post*

98. What Russian writer wrote "Christmas Phantoms," a story about false sentimentality at Christmas?
    a. Maxim Gorki
    b. Alexander Pushkin
    c. Leo Tolstoy
    d. Dr. Zhivago

99. As a young Episcopal priest, Phillips Brooks wrote "O Little Town of Bethlehem" for his Sunday School children. What inspired the hymn?

a. A visit to the Holy Land
b. The nativity scene at his church
c. A drawing by a small boy
d. The children's choir at the annual pageant

100. Which of these Hans Christian Andersen fairy tales takes place at Christmas?

a. "The Little Mermaid"
b. "The Fir Tree"
c. "The Ugly Duckling"
d. "The Tinderbox"

101. Christopher Morley wrote "The Tree that Didn't Get Trimmed." What did this tree become?

    a. A telephone pole
    b. A yule log
    c. A pole for a clothesline
    d. A flagpole

102. E. T. A. Hoffmann wrote the story that became the ballet *The Nutcracker*. Who wrote the music?

    a. Mozart
    b. Tchaikovsky
    c. Rimsky-Korsakov
    d. Baryshnakov

103. In *The Nutcracker,* whom does Clara hit with her shoe?
    a. The Nutcracker
    b. Her little brother
    c. The toy soldier
    d. The Mouse King

104. In Willa Cather's "The Burglar's Christmas," whose house did the burglar try to rob?
    a. Santa Claus's
    b. His own house
    c. His parents'
    d. The preacher's

105. "The Gift of the Magi" was written by O. Henry. What was his real name?
    a. William Sydney Porter
    b. Gene Stratton Porter
    c. O. Henry
    d. Samuel Clemens

106. What does Jim give Della in "The Gift of the Magi"?
    a. A Persian shawl
    b. Tortoise shell combs for her hair
    c. A Christmas cruise
    d. Sweet spices for her plum pudding

107. What is "mumming"?
   a. Keeping Christmas secrets
   b. A stuffing for a goose
   c. Reveling in costumes and masks
   d. The crime of thievery on Christmas Day

108. What was sent from Brant Rock, Massachusetts, on December 24, 1906?
   a. An SOS for the sinking Titanic
   b. The first telegraph signal
   c. The first radio broadcast in the United States
   d. Radio signals to outer space

109. What did a Delaware post office first sell in 1907?
    a. Christmas stamps
    b. Postage to the North Pole
    c. Red-and-green mailing boxes
    d. Christmas Seals

110. Who wrote the poem, "The Journey of the Magi?"

111. Who was the first president not to spend Christmas at the White House, after it was burned in the War of 1812?
    a. James Garfield
    b. Woodrow Wilson
    c. Abraham Lincoln
    d. Dwight Eisenhower

112. A scene of a grandfatherly man trying on a Santa suit on the cover of a December 1916 magazine, launched a tradition. Who was the artist, and what was the magazine?

    a. Thomas Nast and *Life*
    b. Norman Rockwell and *Boys Life*
    c. Howard Finster and *The Watchtower*
    d. Norman Rockwell and *The Saturday Evening Post*

113. Who was president at the first lighting of the national Christmas tree?

    a. Taft
    b. Coolidge
    c. Truman
    d. Dewey

114. What has signaled the beginning of the Christmas season since 1924?
    a. Saint Nicholas's Feast Day
    b. The fall equinox
    c. The Macy's Thanksgiving Day Parade
    d. Christmas decorations in the stores

115. Where did most blown-glass ornaments come from prior to World War II?
    a. Switzerland
    b. Germany
    c. Italy
    d. Japan

116. Whose December advertisements gave us the modern image of Santa?
    a. Coca-Cola
    b. General Electric
    c. Hallmark
    d. Sears Roebuck & Company

117. What is the Christmas census?
    a. Santa's list of boys and girls
    b. A bird count
    c. The law that took Mary and Joseph to Bethlehem
    d. The president's Christmas card list

118. What did as many as one in every ten Americans hold in the 1930s?
    a. Teddy bears
    b. Stock in toy companies
    c. Christmas Club Savings Accounts
    d. Membership in charitable holiday societies

119. Towns in Connecticut, Georgia, Indiana, Iowa, Kentucky, Maryland, Mississippi, New Hampshire, Pennsylvania, and West Virginia share what name?
    a. Christmas
    b. Holiday
    c. Bethlehem
    d. St. Nicholas

120. What American city is nicknamed "The Christmas City"?
a. Galveston, Texas
b. Peoria, Illinois
c. Bethlehem, Pennsylvania
d. La Navidad, New Mexico

121. On Christmas Day, 1931, the Metropolitan Opera broadcast its first opera over the radio. What was the opera?
a. *Aida*
b. *The Messiah*
c. *La Bohème*
d. *Hansel and Gretel*

122. How are "Christmas trees" used in oil wells?
    a. As a "plug"
    b. As a windbreak
    c. As a firebreak
    d. As a decoration

123. When and where was the first Christmas stamp issued?
    a. Delaware in 1907
    b. Russia in 1923
    c. Austria in 1937
    d. The United States in 1945

124. What was Montgomery Ward's 1939 Christmas giveaway?
    a. Christmas stockings
    b. *Rudolph the Red-Nosed Reindeer* books
    c. Fruitcake cookies
    d. Gingerbread men

125. Two towns in the United States are named Santa Claus. Where are they?
    a. Indiana and Illinois
    b. Indiana and Georgia
    c. Georgia and Alabama
    d. Alabama and Illinois

126. What does Ralphie want for Christmas in the movie
A Christmas Story?

a. A yo-yo with red lights
b. A Lionel electric train
c. A Columbia bicycle
d. A Daisy-brand Red Ryder BB gun

127. Which song won the Oscar for Best Song of 1942, and who sang it?
a. "Thanks for the Memories," sung by Bob Hope
b. "White Christmas," sung by Bing Crosby
c. "Silent Night," sung by Bing Crosby
d. "The Secret of Christmas," sung by Bing Crosby

128. In what movie was "White Christmas" first heard?

    a. *Christmas in Connecticut*
    b. *Going My Way*
    c. *Christmas Holiday*
    d. *Holiday Inn*

129. What town in Idaho has a Christmas name? In South Dakota?

130. Which entertainer was not at home for Christmas for twenty-five consecutive years?

131. In what movie did Judy Garland sing the song
     "Have Yourself a Merry Little Christmas"?
     a. *Meet Me in St. Louis*
     b. *Look for the Silver Lining*
     c. *In the Good Old Summertime*
     d. *The Wizard of Oz*

132. Mel Torme and Robert Wells wrote "The Christmas Song"
     in 1946. Who recorded its best-known version?
     a. Bing Crosby
     b. Judy Garland
     c. Nat King Cole
     d. Johnny Ray

133. What is the problem with a "series" type of Christmas light?

134. What is "All I Want for Christmas"?

135. What Texas-born, Oscar-winning actress celebrates a 1949 Christmas birthday?

136. What first lady met her husband-to-be while on Christmas break when she was sixteen years old?
    a. Mamie Eisenhower
    b. Bess Truman
    c. Rosalyn Carter
    d. Barbara Bush

137. Who first recorded the song "Rudolph the
Red-Nosed Reindeer"?
a. Gene Autry
b. Spike Jones
c. Bing Crosby
d. Frank Sinatra

138. "May we keep it in our hearts, that we may be kept
in its hope." This was said of Christmas by whom?
a. Dwight D. Eisenhower
b. Harry Truman
c. Peter Marshall
d. Ebenezer Scrooge

139. What Christmas song did Elvis popularize?
    a. "Jingle Bell Rock"
    b. "I'll Be Home for Christmas"
    c. "Holly Leaves and Christmas Trees"
    d. "Blue Christmas"

140. What present-day organization traces its beginnings to Christmas Eve in 1865?
    a. Order of the Moose
    b. Daughters of the Confederacy
    c. Ku Klux Klan
    d. The Elks

141. Which Christmas carol melody is also known as the state song of Maryland?
    a. "O Christmas Tree"
    b. "The Holly and the Ivy"
    c. "The Cherry Tree Carol"
    d. "O Terra Pin"

142. Here's looking at what 1899 Christmas baby born in New York City?

143. What did Frosty the Snowman have for a nose?

144. Who first recorded the song "Frosty the Snowman"?

145. What is located at North Pole, New York?
    a. Santa's Workshop
    b. Santa's apple cider bottler
    c. Rudolph's birthplace
    d. A sleigh manufacturer

146. On Christmas Eve, 1951, NBC broadcast the first opera written for television. What was it?
    a. *Hansel and Gretel*
    b. *The Little Drummer Boy*
    c. *White Christmas*
    d. *Amahl and the Night Visitors*

147. What are the chances of a white Christmas
in Washington, D.C.?
a. Fifty-fifty
b. One-in-twenty
c. One-in-ten
d. Less than one-in-ten

148. What was invented by an accountant named Carl Otis
in the late 1930s, and was marketed in 1945, but didn't catch
on until the 1950s?
a. Tinker Toys
b. Tinsel icicles
c. Bubble lights
d. Christmas tree scent in cans

149. Bubble lights contained sugar and methyline chloride, a poisonous liquid. What made them bubble?
    a. Neon gas
    b. A low boiling point
    c. Sucrose and sodium chloride
    d. A poltergeist

150. Which president sent the first official Christmas card?
    a. Franklin D. Roosevelt
    b. Dwight D. Eisenhower
    c. John F. Kennedy
    d. Richard M. Nixon

151. What speeded-up recording was a hit in the late 1950s in the children's category?
    a. "The Bow Bow Carol"
    b. "Santa's Busy Toy Shop"
    c. "The Martians' Christmas"
    d. "The Chipmunk Song"

152. Who was Mommy kissing?

153. Who illustrated "The Night Before Christmas" at nearly 100?

154. Which president broadcast his Christmas message from America's first orbiting satellite?

155. What Christmas decorating fad in the 1960s usually included color spotlights?

156. In Truman Capote's "A Christmas Memory," what are the gifts from Buddy and his aunt, and to whom do they want to give one?
    a. Crocheted hot pads and Grandma Moses
    b. Popsicle-stick birdhouses and Boo Radley
    c. Fruitcakes and President Franklin D. Roosevelt
    d. Divinity and the school principal

157. In what year was the first Christmas stamp printed in the
United States?

a. 1942
b. 1952
c. 1962
d. 1972

158. What did the astronauts of Apollo 8 read from space on
Christmas Day, 1969?

159. Who wrote a mystery called
Murder for Christmas?

160. Who was George Bailey's angel?
     a. Dudley
     b. Gabriel
     c. Raphael
     d. Clarence

161. The final sequence of *It's a Wonderful Life* in the original script is slightly different from the ending of the movie. What was omitted?
     a. The Lord's Prayer
     b. Pal, the family mutt
     c. The plum pudding
     d. Kissing under the mistletoe

162. What happens every time a bell rings?

163. Only one presidential Christmas card has featured a photograph. Who was president, and what is the scene?

164. Presidential Christmas cards have contained work by which of the following artists?
    a. N. C. Wyeth
    b. Jamie Wyeth
    c. Mark Hampton
    d. All of the above

165. When did GI Joe hit the stores?
    a. 1959
    b. 1964
    c. 1969
    d. 1974

166. Who narrated the 1964 NBC animated musical "Rudolph the Red-Nosed Reindeer"?
    a. Burl Ives
    b. Truman Capote
    c. Johnny Carson
    d. Jimmy Durante

167. *How the Grinch Stole Christmas* premiered as a television cartoon in 1966. Who was the narrator?
    a. Gene Autry
    b. Burl Ives
    c. Jim Backus
    d. Boris Karloff

168. What was the name of the town in *How the Grinch Stole Christmas*?

169. What is Santa called in France?

170. Who plays the role of Santa in Italy?

171. In what movie did Judy Garland sing "Merry Christmas"?

172. What is Boxing Day and when is it?
     a. World Featherweight Championships, December 22
     b. Australian kangaroo boxing matches, December 25
     c. A gift-giving tradition in England, December 26
     d. The British commemoration of the Boxer Rebellion, December 26

173. *Little Drummer Boy,* an animated television special, premiered in 1967. A sequel, *Drummer Boy II,* premiered in 1976. Who narrated both shows?
     a. Greer Garson
     b. Geraldine Page
     c. Barbara Walters
     d. Carol Channing

174. What oft-married sultry screen star was a Christmas Eve baby in 1922?
    a. Elizabeth Taylor
    b. Ava Gardner
    c. Liz Scott
    d. Sophia Loren

175. What modern inventor and millionaire recluse was born on December 24?

176. What popular series was spawned by the 1971 holiday television production of *The Homecoming*, a story by Earl Hamner, Jr.?

177. Who said, "The only real blind person at Christmas time is he who has not Christmas in his heart"?
    a. Ray Charles
    b. Helen Keller
    c. John Milton
    d. Charlie Boswell

178. In the tenth century, a duke in Bohemia was murdered by his brother and later canonized. What is he called today?
    a. Dracula
    b. Good King Wenceslaus
    c. Saint Nikolai
    d. Saint Christmas

179. What modern poet's Christmas memories began as a radio script for the BBC and eventually became a television drama?

    a. Dylan Thomas
b. T. S. Eliot
c. Ogden Nash
d. Robert Frost

180. What does the X stand for in Xmas?

    a. It is a mark denying religious aspects of the holiday.
b. Unknown
c. Messiah
d. The Greek letter Chi

181. What Supreme Court case impacted the observance of Christmas?

    a. *Lynch v. Donnelly*
    b. *Marbury v. Madison*
    c. *Brown v. Board of Education*
    d. *American Civil Liberties Union v. City of Schenectady*

182. What did my true love give me on the tenth day of Christmas?

183. What 1984 toy was one of the biggest all-time sellers?

184. What is a "Christmas tree" in CB jargon?

185. What is a "Christmas card" in CB jargon?

186. How is "Merry Christmas" written in Sweden?
    a. Noelinz Ve Yeni Yiliniz Kutlu Olsun
    b. Een Plesierige Kerfees
    c. Boldog Karacsony
    d. Glad Jul

187. What 1973 animated television special features Tom Smothers as a bear?
    a. *Baby Bear and Goldilocks at Christmas*
    b. *Pooh-Bear's Gift for Santa*
    c. *The Bear Who Slept through Christmas*
    d. *This Was the Bear That Was*

188. Why were world maps redrawn following Christmas Day, 1991?
    a. The United Nations sent peacekeeping troops to Africa,
       Bosnia, and Malaysia.
    b. India annexed five neighboring countries.
    c. The Soviet Union disintegrated.
    d. Rand McNally Atlas Company lost its copyrights.

189. What happened to Grandma?
    a. She got tipsy eating fruitcake.
    b. She got run over by a reindeer.
    c. The department store Santa kissed her.
    d. She won the jackpot on the slot machine.

190. What 1985 toy talked and sang while cash registers rang up $93 million in sales?

191. What plant commonly used as a Christmas decoration is poisonous?

192. Who plays the role of Santa in Russia?

    a. Saint Basil
    b. Black Peter
    c. Babouschka
    d. No one

193. What Christmas song comes from the Bob Hope movie, *The Lemon Drop Kid?*
    a. "Hunka Hunka Christmas Chocolate"
    b. "The Christmas Song"
    c. "I'll Have a Blue Christmas Without You"
    d. "Silver Bells"

194. The longest-reigning monarch of modern times began his reign on Christmas Day. Who was the monarch?
    a. Haile Selassie of Ethiopia
    b. Hirohito of Japan
    c. Kalakaua of Tuvalu
    d. The Sultan of Brunei

195. What did the king of France give Henry III of England for Christmas in 1236?
    a. Defeat on the battlefield
    b. Sillabub

    c. A live elephant
    d. A ruby for his crown

196. How many Oscars did *It's a Wonderful Life* win?
    a. None
    b. Five
    c. Seven
    d. Eight

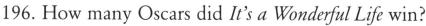

197. Who joined President Roosevelt at the 1941 lighting
    of the National Christmas Tree?
    a. Billy Graham
    b. Cardinal Francis Joseph Spellman
    c. Father Flanagan
    d. Winston Churchill

198. Why was the National Christmas Tree lit for only 6 minutes
    and 57 seconds in 1980?
    a. The power company went on strike.
    b. To remember the hostages in Iran
    c. To emphasize the energy crisis
    d. There was a power failure on Pennsylvania Avenue.

199. What is Christmas Ridge?

200. What did Linus read in "A Charlie Brown Christmas"?
    a. The Christmas story from Luke's Gospel
    b. "The Night Before Christmas"
    c. His lines from the school Christmas play
    d. A recipe for the Christmas punch

ANSWERS

1. (b) A.D. 336 is the date at which December 25 shows up as the Feast of the Nativity on the Calendar of the Church of Rome, although there is evidence that December 25 was observed as early as A.D. 98.

2. (d) Turkey. The real Saint Nicholas was an early Christian bishop in Myra in southwest Asia Minor. Today the town is the little village of Demre in Turkey.

3. (b) The middle fourth century A.D.

4. The Bible mentions no animals. They were added later by artists and writers.

5. Micah, in chapter five, verse two

6. (c) Diocletian persecuted Christians and is said to have killed 20,000 on

Christmas Day in the year 303. Constantine, who succeeded him as ruler, was the first Christian emperor.

7. (a) 4 B.C. Although "B.C." means Before Christ, scholars reckon the year to be 4 B.C. Herod, who died in 2 B.C., was ruler when Christ was born.

8. (c) Gabriel, the Bearer of Good News, is one of four archangels named in the Bible. The others are Michael, Uriel, and Raphael.

9. (b) Matthew 1:18-2:12 and Luke 2:1-20

10. (d) Melchior, Balthasaar, and Kaspar, according to legend. The names are first found in a sixth century Armenian writing.

11. (b) Saturnalia, which marked the winter solstice. It honored Saturn, the god of agriculture, as the solstice marks the return of the sun to the sky and the return of the growing season. It was a time of gift-

giving and great festivity. Many other pagan cultures observed the solstice with great rituals.

12. The Bible does not give a number. In early Christianity the number varied from two to six. Three, the traditional number, is probably related to the three gifts of gold, frankincense, and myrrh.

13. December 25 through January 6. While the Western part of the Church chose December 25, the Eastern part of the Church observed Christ's coming into the world at the same time as the feast of His manifestation, or Epiphany, on January 6. Epiphany marks Christ's baptism, the visit of the Magi, and Christ's first miracle. By the sixth century the Eastern part of the Church joined the West in separately observing Christ's birth on December 25. Since the entire Church continued to celebrate Epiphany, this entire period made up the "Twelve Days of Christmas."

14. (d) All of the above

15. Germany

16. (c) Greece and Russia

17. (b) He gave them each a dowry. As the story goes, a nobleman had lost his fortune, leaving his three daughters with no dowries. Saint Nicholas slipped past their house late at night and tossed three bags of gold into an open window, making the three girls eligible to marry. Saint Nicholas has since been portrayed carrying three gold balls or bags of gold.

18. (a) An aromatic resin used in burials

19. (c) A festival. Often the festival lasted twelve days, though it was not associated then with the twelve days of Christmas.

20. (c) Adapt them to the praise of God. Gregory, who was later canonized, advised Christendom to absorb many of the customs and use them to God's glory. Consequently, candles, evergreens, mistletoe, yule logs, and gift giving have become part of Christmas.

21. (b) His bones were moved from Turkey to Bari, Italy, which became the destination of many pilgrimages.

22. (d) King Arthur, who on December 25, 521, celebrated his victory at York with the Knights of the Round Table.

23. (a) It touches the ground. Important in mythology and ceremonial rites in northern Europe, mistletoe was thought to have magical and medicinal properties.

24. Holly represents the crown of thorns, while the red berries represent droplets of the blood of Christ.

25. A large log, preferably oak or fruitwood, that will burn slowly. It must burn or smolder for the Twelve Days of Christmas, leaving a piece large enough to light the next year's fire.

26. A beverage, the contents of which vary. Today it is a drink of ale or spiced wine with apples and sugar. The recipe once included mulled ale, beaten eggs, curdled cream, roasted apples, nuts, sugar, and spices.

27. (c) "Be well" or "Be in good health." The response: "Drink well."

28. Asking for a sign to reveal their rightful king, Merlin called together the leaders of the realm on Christmas Day to remove a sword embedded in an anvil. As only Arthur could free the sword, he gained his right to rule as king.

29. (a) December 6 is the feast day of Saint Nicholas, noting the anniversary of his death around A.D. 345-352 in Asia Minor. In many countries this is the day children expect gifts from Saint Nick.

30. William the Conqueror was crowned King of England.

31. (c) Saint Francis of Assisi received the pope's permission in 1223 to set up a nativity scene using live people and animals in the little village of Greccio, near Assisi in Italy. Crowds came to hear him conduct the services, thus launching the manger scene as a Christmas tradition.

32. (b) Lucia Della Robbia invented enameled terra cotta sculptures, which were affordable for the rising middle class. The enameled ware made by the Della Robbia family is still popular today.

33. (d) Named a port in Haiti. Having wrecked the *Santa Maria* on a coral reef, Columbus transferred to the *Niña* and sailed into a port in what is now Haiti. He named the port La Navidad, or The Nativity.

34. (c) Martin Luther

35. (d) *The Mystic Nativity*

36. (a) "Christmas" is mentioned only three times.

37. (b) *Hamlet.* This is the only passage in Shakespeare's plays in which Christmas is discussed as a topic rather than as a date.

38. (b) His copy of "Aristotle." The student had to cut off the boar's head to retrieve his book. When he brought the head to the dinner table, the annual Queens College tradition of serving a boar's head for Christmas began.

39. (b) Christmas was illegal. The Puritans under Oliver Cromwell considered Christmas merrymaking a heathen custom, so Parliament passed an act forbidding the celebration of Christmas and Easter. People could not light Christmas candles or eat cake, and shops were required to stay open.

40. (c) Sir Isaac Newton

41. Advent, or the advent season, a time of spiritual preparation for Christmas

42. Stuck in his thumb and pulled out a plum. This nursery rhyme is based on a story from the time of Henry VIII of England about a church official who acquired the "plum" of a deed to a manor.

43. "The Boar's Head Carol" was part of a collection printed in England in 1521 by Jan Wynken de Worde that may have been the first printed music in England.

44. (a) Cutting trees. They worked as on any other day. Still living aboard the Mayflower, they went ashore to cut trees for houses. The Puritans did not believe in celebrations or observe the Christmas season, as it was not a biblical holiday.

45. (c) "While Shepherds Watched Their Flocks." The melody is from Handel's opera *Siroe.* The carol's lyrics were written by Nahum Tate, a British dramatist and poet who became poet laureate of England and wrote a version of King Lear with a happy ending.

46. (a) According to legend, when Saint Nicholas tossed bags of gold into a window for three penniless girls to use as dowries, the bags landed in their stockings, which had been hung by the fire to dry. Thus began the worldwide custom of Santa leaving gifts in stockings or shoes.

47. (b) Thieves. Saint Nicholas had been imprisoned, so he was acquaint-ed with thieves, who took him as their patron saint even though he made them return what they had stolen.

48. (d) Saint Nicholas is portrayed carrying three gold balls, which repre-sent three bags of gold he gave to three sisters in need of dowries. The three balls came to be the universal symbol of moneylenders.

49. (b) German Protestant churches. Kris Kringle is another name for Saint Nicholas, a name derived from Christkind, meaning Christ child.

50. (b) "Joy to the World." A Congregationalist minister from England, Isaac Watts, wrote this hymn. Watts and Charles Wesley, brother of John Wesley, would go on to become the most prolific hymn writers in English history.

51. (a) Johann Sebastian Bach. The oratorio is a set of six cantatas that tell the Christmas story as found in Matthew and Luke.

52. (c) Saint Nicholas, according to Washington Irving in his history of the Dutch in New York

53. (a) Charles Wesley, in 1739. He wrote more than 6,500 hymns during his lifetime.

54. (d) George Fredrick Handel's *The Messiah,* with its "Hallelujah Chorus"

55. (b) Crossed the Delaware River. Knowing he might catch the Hessian troops asleep after too much Christmas revelry, General Washington crossed the Delaware River in New Jersey and took them by surprise, thus winning the Battle of Trenton. This was a turning point in the Revolutionary War.

56. (a) Toy soldiers. They were made of metal, dressed in colorful uniforms, and cost 18 shillings a dozen.

57. (d) The Methodist Church was formed at the Christmas Conference, a Baltimore convocation in 1784. Thomas Coke and Francis Asbury were joint superintendents.

58. (c) John Adams, with his wife, Abigail, and daughter, Suzanna, experienced a frigid holiday in 1800. There was a hole in the White House roof, and Adams had just learned that he lost his bid for re-election.

59. (a) Washington Irving, in 1809, in *Diedrich Knickerbocker's History of New York from the Beginning of the World to the End of the Dutch Dynasty*

60. (c) The Treaty of Ghent, signed in Belgium in 1814, ended the War of 1812 between Britain and the United States. The Battle of New Orleans was fought after the war was officially over, as the news of the treaty took six weeks to reach General Andrew Jackson and his British counterpart.

61. (a) Kit Carson, a scout along the Oregon Trail and a famed Indian fighter in the Southwest, was born in Madison, Kentucky.

62. (c) The carol "Silent Night." Joseph Mohr, the priest, quickly wrote lyrics for the song, and Franz Gruber, the organist, hurriedly put them to music. That night "Silent Night! Holy Night!" was sung for the first time.

63. (d) Clement C. Moore, a professor of divinity in New York City, wrote the poem for his children in December of 1822. It was published anonymously as "A Visit from St. Nicholas" in the *Troy Sentinel* on December 23, 1823.

64. (a) None. He calls him Saint Nicholas, although variations of Santa were being used when Moore wrote the poem.

65. Dasher, Dancer, Prancer, Vixen, Comet, Cupid, Donder, Blitzen, and Rudolph

66. His belly shook like a bowl full of jelly.

67. Sugar plums

68. (a) Mexico

69. (d) The name came from a United States diplomat, Dr. Joel R. Poinsett of South Carolina. An avid botanist, he introduced the plant to the United States while serving as minister to Mexico in the 1820s.

70. (c) It is the birth date of founder Clara Barton, a philanthropist and Civil War nurse who became the first president of the American Red Cross in 1881. She served until 1904.

71. (b) A song to dance to. Probably derived from the Greek choraules, carols were not necessarily religious songs.

72. (b) London in 1843. Sir Henry Cole had his friend, the artist John Calcott Horsley, design the cards. One thousand were printed on

cardboard and hand painted. They depicted a family toasting an absent friend with the words, "A Merry Christmas and a Happy New Year to You." The side panels showed the poor receiving gifts.

73. (c) Prince Albert, the German-born husband of Queen Victoria, brought the tradition with him from Germany. A picture of the royal family gathered around their decorated tree appeared in the *Illustrated London News* in 1848. Almost at once, every English family had a Christmas tree.

74. (d) Alabama, in 1836.

75. Jacob Marley. Marley's spirit is the first of four ghosts to appear to Ebenezer Scrooge on Christmas Eve.

76. (b) Fezziwig. The Ghost of Christmas Past takes Scrooge back in time to his employment by jolly Mr. Fezziwig and the lively Christmas ball at Fezziwig's warehouse.

77. (c) A goose

78. (a) "Jingle Bells." Written in 1857 by James Pierpont, it didn't become a popular Christmas song until the twentieth century. Originally it was called "One Horse Open Sleigh."

79. (c) "We Three Kings." This hymn, written by John Henry Hopkins Jr. in 1857, is one of only a few written about the wise men.

80. (b) Abraham Lincoln. There was no "standard" image of Santa until Nast, at Lincoln's request, began a series of illustrations for *Harper's Illustrated Weekly* in 1863. Nast relied on Clement Moore's description for his Santa.

81. (a) Cartoonist Thomas Nast created the donkey and elephant as political symbols, and he is credited with creating our image of Santa as a jolly, bearded little fellow dressed in red.

82. (c) Franklin Pierce, in 1856

83. (c) "I Heard the Bells on Christmas Day." Longfellow's son, a young lieutenant in the Union Army, had been seriously wounded. The poem is about the anguish of war.

84. (c) Savannah, Georgia. After burning his way across the South, General Sherman reached the sea at Savannah on December 22 and sent Lincoln a telegram saying: "I beg to present you, as a Christmas gift, the city of Savannah."

85. (b) It freely mixes English and Latin. "The Boar's Head Carol" is an example.

86. Lowing

87. (c) "O Holy Night." On Christmas Eve, while the French and the Germans faced each other in the trenches, a young French soldier

suddenly stood and sang, "O Holy Night." Silence followed. Then a German soldier responded with Martin Luther's Christmas hymn, "From Heaven above I Come to You."

88. "Greensleeves"

89. (b) The vice president of Thomas Edison's electric light company, Edward H. Johnson, wired the tree in his home with blinking lights in three colors. He also wired a stand to make the tree rotate. The date was 1882.

90. (a) Grover Cleveland

91. (c) Angel's hair, or billowing gossamer strands, were produced as Christmas decorations in Germany in the 1880s.

92. (d) Louis Prang, a German immigrant and lithographer in Roxbury, Massachusetts, began producing Christmas cards in 1874.

93. (c) Thomas Nast drew a cartoon in 1882 for *Harper's Weekly* showing Santa sitting on a box addressed "Christmas Box 1882, St. Nicholas, North Pole."

94. (b) "America the Beautiful"

95. (d) Cutting off his left earlobe. After quarreling with his friend Paul Gaugin, Van Gogh cut off part of his left ear. The two had left Paris for Arles in the South of France. They hoped to start a colony of impressionist painters.

96. (a) *Hansel and Gretel.* The opera, which debuted just before Christmas in 1893 at Weimar, Germany, was immediately popular. The fairy tale and its gingerbread house blended well with images of the Christmas season.

97. (b) *The New York Sun* first carried the famous reply to eight-year-old Virginia O'Hanlon's question, "Is there a Santa Claus?", in 1897. It was reprinted each Christmas until the paper closed in 1949.

98. (a) Maxim Gorki. An author is visited in a dream by tragic characters he has sprinkled throughout his stories for effect.

99. (a) A visit to the Holy Land

100. (b) "The Fir Tree" is a story about a tree that thinks being a Christmas tree would be preferable to simply living in the forest. Only one other Hans Christian Andersen fairy tale takes place during the Christmas season, although "The Little Match Girl" takes place on New Year's Eve.

101. (c) A pole for a clothesline

102. (b) The Russian composer Peter Ilich Tchaikovsky, in 1891. The story was translated from German into French by Alexandre Dumas, who wrote *The Three Musketeers*.

103. (d) The Mouse King. He is addled by the hit, and the battle turns against him.

104. (c) His parents'

105. (a) William Sydney Porter

106. (b) He sold his watch to buy tortoise shell combs for her beautiful long hair. Meanwhile, she had sold her long hair to buy him a chain for his watch.

107. (c) Reveling, merrymaking, and parading in costumes and masks, sometimes with men dressed as women. The practice dates back to the Roman Saturnalia, when all rules were set aside and customs were turned upside down. Philadelphia's annual Mummers Day Parade is modern-day mumming.

108. (c) The first known radio broadcast in the United States. Using an experimental station, Reginald A. Fessenden presented a Christmas Eve program of music, including a violin solo and a speech.

109. (d) Christmas Seals, as a means to raise money to fight tuberculosis, a leading cause of death in the country at that time. The custom, which originated in Denmark, was introduced here by a Danish immigrant, Jacob Riis, a philanthropist and editor who had lost six brothers to tuberculosis.

110. T.S. Eliot.

111. (b) Woodrow Wilson, who spent Christmas in 1913 on a vacation in Mississippi and in 1915 on his honeymoon at the Homestead in Hot Springs, Virginia. He and Edith Galt were married on December 18, 1915.

112. (d) Norman Rockwell and *The Saturday Evening Post*

113. (b) Calvin Coolidge, who in 1923 turned on the lights on a sixty-foot-high cut fir provided by Middlebury College of Vermont on the Ellipse side of the White House. The Society for Electrical

Development footed the costs of power and publicity to encourage the new trend of using outdoor lights.

114. (c) The Macy's Thanksgiving Day Parade. In 1924 the R. H. Macy Company in New York City opened a twenty-story department store and organized the parade to launch the season. The parade has become an annual tradition.

115. (b) A tiny village in Germany in the Thuringian Mountains called Lauscha. The glass-making industry flourished in Lauscha from the 1590s until World War II.

116. (a) Coca-Cola, beginning in 1931 with a series of Santa paintings by illustrator Haddon Sundblom. His Santa was the jolly, fat fellow in red, but was also grandfatherly, tall, and robust. Santa was fully human, no longer an elf.

117. (b) An annual count of wintering birds first organized by the National Audubon Society. Volunteers in each state annually make a dawn-to-dusk observation of a fifteen-mile diameter circle, recording the habitats of as many birds as possible.

118. (c) Christmas Club Savings Accounts. Depositors set aside a set amount each week until two weeks before Christmas, when the money was returned to them. Started in Carlisle, Pennsylvania, in 1905, the clubs eventually spread to 8,000 banks.

119. (c) Bethlehem. South Africa and the Virgin Islands also have cities named Bethlehem.

120. (c) Bethlehem, Pennsylvania, about 50 miles north of Philadelphia on the Lehigh River, was originally settled by the Moravians on Christmas Eve, 1741.

121. (d) *Hansel and Gretel*

122. (a) As a "plug." Oil in an oil well seldom flows to the surface spontaneously. If it does, a series of valves, gauges, and chokes, called a Christmas tree, is constructed on the surface to control the flow.

123. (c) Austria in 1937. The stamp featured a rose, a popular Christmas symbol in that country. Brazil followed two years later with the first religious Christmas stamp, which featured a nativity scene.

124. (b) The story of *Rudolph the Red-Nosed Reindeer.* Robert L. May, a copywriter for Montgomery Ward and Company, wrote Rudolph's story as a booklet for store Santas to hand out. The store passed out 2.4 million copies in 1939, and 3.6 million when it was used again in 1946.

125. (b) Indiana and Georgia

126. (d) It was a Daisy-brand Red Ryder repeating BB carbine with a compass mounted in the stock—the dream of every boy in the 1940s.

127. (b) "White Christmas," sung by Bing Crosby

128. (d) *Holiday Inn.* The song became the best-selling record of all time, so the movie was remade as *White Christmas*, again featuring the voice of Bing Crosby, in 1954.

129. Santa, Idaho; Epiphany, South Dakota

130. Bob Hope, who spent each Christmas entertaining American soldiers at home and abroad

131. (a) *Meet Me in St. Louis*

132. (c) Nat King Cole

133. When one light goes out, the whole strand goes out.

134. "My Two Front Teeth." This Spike Jones song was the first major-selling novelty Christmas record.

135. Sissy Spacek, who won an Oscar for Best Actress in *Coal Miner's Daughter* and starred in *The River*, was born in Quitman, Texas, on December 25, 1949.

136. (d) Barbara Pierce met George Bush in Connecticut in 1941 while she was on Christmas vacation from Ashley Hall in South Carolina. She attended Smith College while he was in the Navy during World War II, and they married when he returned in 1944.

137. (a) Gene Autry, the "singing cowboy," in 1949

138. (c) Peter Marshall, a Presbyterian minister who served as chaplain of the United States Senate. The movie *A Man Called Peter* was the story of his life.

139. (d) "Blue Christmas"

140. (c) Ku Klux Klan. Confederate veterans formed the organization in Pulaski, Tennessee.

141. (a) "O Christmas Tree"

142. Humphrey Bogart. An actor on stage and screen, Bogie is best remembered for his roles in *Casablanca, The African Queen,* and *The Maltese Falcon.* He died January 14, 1957.

143. A carrot

144. Gene Autry

145. (a) Santa's Workshop is a theme park open since 1949 near Lake Placid in Wilmington. It has its own post office designated as North Pole.

146. (d) *Amahl and the Night Visitors.* NBC commissioned Gian Carlo Menotti to write the opera about a poor mother and her crippled son who were visited by the three kings on their way to Bethlehem.

147. (d) Less than one-in-ten, according to the U.S. Weather Service

148. (c) Bubble lights for Christmas trees

149. (b) A low boiling point

150. (b) Dwight D. Eisenhower in 1953

151. (d) "The Chipmunk Song (Christmas Don't Be Late)"

152. Santa Claus underneath the mistletoe, according to the 1952 hit song, "I Saw Mommy Kissing Santa Claus"

153. Grandma Moses. Anna Mary Robertson Moses did the drawings in 1960 at the invitation of Bennett Cerf and Random House. Grandma Moses was born in 1860 and died in 1961.

154. Dwight D. Eisenhower, in 1958

155. Aluminum trees. The trees were shiny with pompons at the tip of each branch. Ranging in size from two and one-half to eight feet tall, they sold for $2.29 to $22.49. They usually were decorated with balls of only one color.

156. (c) Fruitcakes and President Franklin D. Roosevelt

157. (c) 1962. The red-and-green stamp pictured a Christmas wreath and candles.

158. Genesis 1.

159. Agatha Christie

160. (d) Clarence, in *It's A Wonderful Life*.

161. (a) The Lord's Prayer. In the original, Uncle Billy dropped to his knees and began the prayer. Gradually everyone in the room joined him.

162. An angel gets his wings. (from *It's a Wonderful Life*)

163. John F. Kennedy. The Kennedy's 1962 Christmas card shows Jackie, Caroline, and John John riding in a sleigh drawn by the children's pony, Macaroni, over the snow-covered South Lawn of the White House.

164. (d) All of the above

165. (b) In 1964, GI Joe was available as a U.S. Army soldier, a U.S. Navy sailor, a U.S. Marine, and a U.S. Air Force pilot.

166. (a) Burl Ives

167. (d) Boris Karloff

168. Who-ville

169. Pére Noel, or Father Christmas

170. La Befana, a good witch, who wanted to join the wise men on their journey

171. *In the Good Old Summertime* (1949)

172. (c) December 26 is called Boxing Day in England because of the old custom of giving remembrances in Christmas boxes to servants and those who perform public service.

173. (a) Greer Garson

174. (b) Ava Gardner, who starred in *The Barefoot Contessa* and *The Night of the Iguana*. She was married to Mickey Rooney, Artie Shaw, and Frank Sinatra.

175. Howard Hughes, inventor, flier, and film producer, was born in 1905. He died a recluse in 1976.

176. "The Waltons." The original production stars Patricia Neal and Richard Thomas.

177. (b) Helen Keller

178. (b) Good King Wenceslaus

179. (a) Dylan Thomas, who wrote *A Child's Christmas in Wales*

180. (d) The Greek letter Chi, the first letter in Christ's name, has always been a symbol for Christ. Xmas has been used as an abbreviation for Christmas since the twelfth century.

181. (a) *Lynch v. Donnelly* (465 U.S. 668). The court found that Pawtucket, Rhode Island, could place a nativity scene on public property without infringing on the principles of separation of church and state. The court was split in the 1984 decision, as have been leaders within both the Christian and Jewish faiths.

182. Ten pipers piping

183. Cabbage Patch Kids. They made their creator, Xavier Roberts, a multi-millionaire.

184. A truck with a lot of bright lights

185. A traffic ticket

186. (d) Glad Jul. The other answers are "Merry Christmas" (a) in Turkey, (b) for Afrikaans of South Africa, and (c) in Hungary.

187. (c) *The Bear Who Slept through Christmas* was about a bear who did not want to hibernate, and thus missed Christmas.

188. (c) Mikhail Gorbachev resigned as premier of the Soviet Union. Boris Yeltsin took over, and the Soviet Union broke up into independent republics.

189. (b) "Grandma Got Run Over By a Reindeer" in Elmo 'n Patsy's song.

190. Teddy Ruxpin, a bear with a concealed microchip, manufactured by Worlds of Wonder

191. Holly berries

192. (c) Babouschka. Like La Befana in Italy, Babouschka is a good witch who wanted to go with the wise men to visit the baby Jesus when she finished her sweeping, but they would not wait for her. She still carries her broom and searches for the Christ child.

193. (d) "Silver Bells"

194. (b) Hirohito of Japan became emperor on December 25, 1926, and reigned for more than 62 years until his death early in 1989.

195. (c) A live elephant

196. (a) None, although it was nominated for five. The film was a commercial failure, and wound up in the red. Its great popularity began in 1973 when nearly every television station in the country began using it in their holiday programming.

197. (d) Winston Churchill

198. (b) To remember the American hostages being held in Iran, the tree remained dark in 1979. A relative of one of the hostages persuaded President Carter to light the tree on Christmas Eve in 1980, allowing one second for each of the 417 hostages—a total of 6 minutes and 57 seconds.

199. An underwater mountain chain located in the Pacific Ocean near Hawaii

200. (a) The Christmas story from Luke's Gospel